Four Corners of Depression

For information address:
J2B Publishing LLC
4251 Columbia Park Road
Pomfret, MD 20675
www.J2BLLC.com

Cover and photos by Dave Stant

Printed and bound in the United States of America.

This book is set in Garamond.

ISBN: 978-1-954682-04-7

Four Corners of Depression

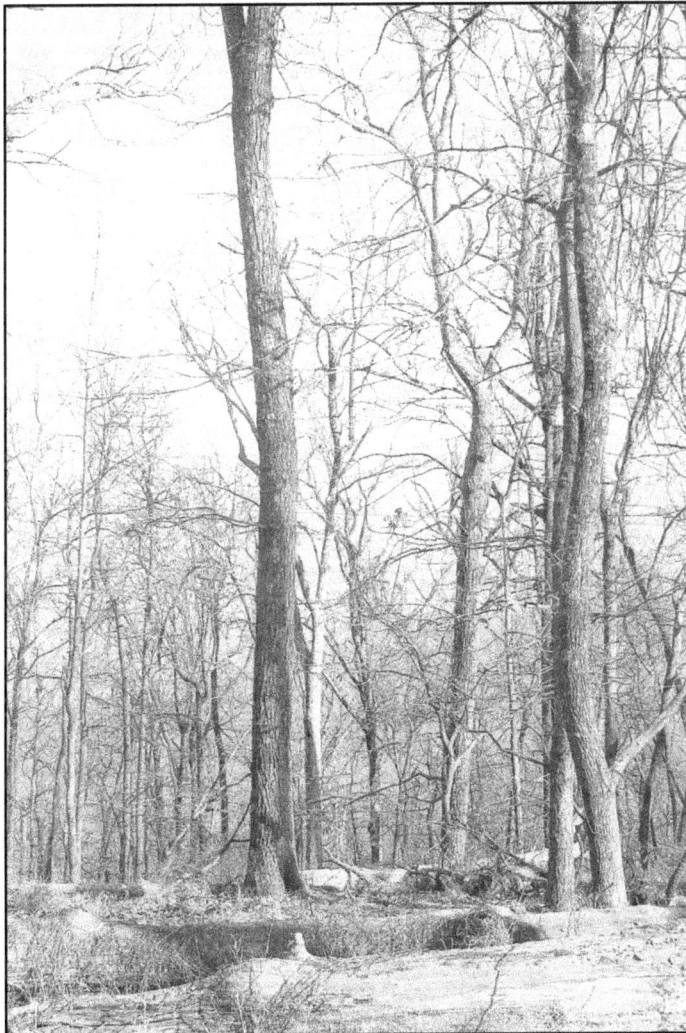

Dave Stant

J2B PUBLISHING

Contents

Visualization Exercise

Imagine yourself sitting in the middle of a magical room.

When you entered, you were told that after you look into a corner, if you look back, you will have the same experience.

In the first corner you look, the ground begins to cave in and you feel yourself slipping through the cracks. In the next corner, everything turns to gray, and your mood becomes somber. In the third, you see a picture of the bright yellow sun, but there are clouds moving toward it. You pause and accept this scenery as truth. In the final corner, the room appears for the most part unblemished. There is dust and chipped paint on the wall, but you're relieved that you've returned to a level of normalcy. Now you are able to stand on your feet and walk out of the room.

In my case, this is the experience of depression. It is important to know that healing is possible. Remember that mental illness is not a battle that can be won. Without proper treatment, it can be life ending. With proper treatment, life ebbs and flows as it does for everyone, only more intensely.

The Devil Creeps In

I step outside
A voice calls down to me from a cloudy sky
"Let me tell you a story about a boy who lied"

Not long after, lying fearful in a comfortable bed,
Finding truth in the wise intonation of the words spoken,
Demonic voices begin to appear in my head,

Threatening with serpent tones and the truth that follow,
Life slipping through palms sweat wet from the sweltering
heat,
I fall asleep empty and hollow,

Waking in a dreamscape reality,
Blurring edges between truth and fantasy,
Not able to claim my sanity

The season turns to fall
Cold shoulders cut sharp like razors through my jacket
Creating wounds that refuse to heal

With the onset of mental illness, those suffering often believe there are spiritual underpinnings to their experience. While this is a poem about depression, the language used accurately portrays my perception of what was taking place.

Broken

My brain has been bleeding for months
My beating heart has become brittle

My mind has submerged under water
If the pain continues like glass I may break
Friends reach out a hand but I'm convinced its fake

I lash out in a fit of rage
Fall to the floor then climb to my knees in shame
The floodgates break then tears fall like rain

They take me to a safe place
They tell me its for the best
I tried to do right and created a mess

A few days feels like an eternity when your soul is torn
I return home before the week is over.....

6

They Tell Me Lies

Hope lingers like love out of reach
Once uplifting now only lies they speak
Every friend lurking in the shadows stalking like a creep

Am I out of touch?
Every lie I question
People tell me this is a blessing
My soul burns slowly embers turning to ash

Searching for a new beginning
I don't succeed and again I try
I spend days thinking of a disguise
To avoid laceration my will shatters like glass

This inner death I swallow with pills at bedtime
Until my memories become lies too.

When I first returned to college, everything seemed unattainable, and my trust had been completely shattered. Even my own memories became lies to me. This poem highlights the dark cloud that hovers over a person's interpretation of events in the beginning of the journey toward recovery.

Into the Ashes

I walk the shoulder of a highway
I've fallen into the depths of hell
I attempted to rise like a phoenix
Into the ashes my body fell

I intended to leave this Earth
Not with a bang but with a whimper
The police draw their weapons,
They yell, "Get down on the ground!"

I left my home with nowhere to run
Like Icarus my sights were set to close to the sun
My body hits the ground as if it weighs a ton

The doctors say it may never be the same
The spirit of life leaves through a bleeding heart
A familiar sting from the piercing cold air

Dear God

Dear God,

Is this punishment or without a cause?
Doesn't my problem break a natural law?
Infinite beauty cannot be seen if a link is broken

How could you burden me with so much pain?
Did I live my life in vain?
When a cross to bear is given stones are thrown

When gravity intensifies and I feel weak
My mind is active but my mouth won't speak
And through a kaleidoscope I see a projection of the future

I try with heart and strength to find my path
In time I will be in recovery at last
For now I must walk alone

When I began to put a plan together for my life again, I couldn't justify the existence of God without the belief that I was being punished for something I had done. Hence, my course in life was forever altered.

I Went to a Party

I went to a party with a mask
And wore it to hide the truth behind my smile
I blame each grievance to make my life worthwhile
You're all alone when everyone's an enemy

I went to a party to a have a drink
So no one will see my expression
It will drive me to the brink in my next therapy session
I've heard a feast can be made from crumbs

I went to a party to meet new friends
To hide a face needing to be seen
There are two worlds I exist between
Truth hurts but truth heals

I want desperately to spread my arms toward the sky
Let loose and relieve all of the stress
To have a woman be impressed
But I feel like walking into the ocean leaving the beach
behind

Life for me returned to normal fairly quickly. However, my world on the inside did not match the image I was projecting. I remember nights spent at clubs feeling like I was dying on the inside.

The Lies We Tell

I tell myself a lie,
A serpent's fangs have not pierced my skin
I'll not fall into the fiery pit of hell
I exist as glue between friends that I bind

I tell myself a lie,
I project the image of perfection
My life merely needs revisions
A deadly poison has not entered my mind

I tell myself a lie,
I've not wandered into the desert
Into the distance is not an illusion
O'er the horizon riches and treasure I shall find

Still I tell myself lies.......

*The most difficult part of recovery after surviving the first crash is acceptance.
Denial comes in many forms and tells many lies. A person must accept that a
struggle exists before being able to overcome the struggle.*

3 AM Thoughts

A breeze blows through the open window
Resting next to the poet's desk
A tired soul returned from the corner bar
Awakens half drunk at 2 AM
To capture the emotions that called him forth

To happiness, he says, don't say goodbye
I've chased you tirelessly
Down the neighborhood streets
Each leading only to the other
And to faith, he says, I blame you
I've cried and prayed, fought and hoped
With a broken heart and broken bones

He remembers the words, a happenstance thought,
That occurred in his drunken, dimly lit mind
The light in the poet's mind flickers
And from his consciousness to the page
"Faith is like happiness
The harder one chases it,
The harder it is to find"

Seasonal Affective

After my psychiatrist found the correct medication, and my therapist applied the correct treatment, I spent the next ten years changing with the beginning and passing of each season. In fall, the expectations of summer recede, and I transition to a view that much of life seems bleak. Winter's colder weather and endless nights bring about a sadness I can't rid myself of. The beginning of spring creates inspiration and leads to a more positive outlook. In summer, life is happening everywhere, and I feel alive. The next four poems invite you to experience the same feelings as I do as each season comes and goes.

Touch of the Season

(Mood Poem- Fall)

The graceful touch of the season.......

Autumnal hues of brown, orange, and yellow
Dangle from tree branches
Descending slowly at first
Best seen having one's first breath
Of the crisp, cooling evening air
The temperature drops slowly
Reminding me of empty promises
Cold rains fall under a gray cloudy sky

The Moonlight Cries

(Mood Poem- Winter)

Moonlight shines through the clouds
Light illuminates her deep brown eyes
I taste the bitterness of a cold winter's frost
She reaches out the palm of her hand,
Touching me softly on my cheek
I hold back a swell of tears,
High tide brings winter's cold breeze
Her eyes tell the story,
This would be our final goodbye

This poem is dedicated to my best friend Nicole. Every summer, we would talk of going to the beach. Before long, winter would arrive.

Flowers Under the Sun

(Mood Poem- Spring)

I gaze upon the flowers,
Smelling sweet scents of hopefulness,
Sad their friendship only appears on sunny days;
Adversity is a narrow mountain pass,
Though a valley of life's hues awaits;
New beginnings speak to the beauty within,
So many colors having spent seasons in hiding;
I'm looking forward to whats to come,
Like the budding flowers under the sun

City Lights

(Mood Poem- Summer)

I look out at the city lights,
Appearing like stars painted on a black canvas;
My soul is stolen from the summer sun
Rhythms of truth speed past crowded streets,
Lovers play the melody of the city's heartstrings,
The city is man's creation,
From which comes the beauty that I see,
Slowly I begin to realize,
What is possible for me to achieve

Turning the Corner

It wasn't until I accepted that my life would have to change
that I was able to turn the corner in my recovery. I began to
wish that somewhere in the vast wasteland that had become
my life I would find a place within an increasingly
complicated time. For the first time, a light shined in an
unexpected way when I met Cristl, and we shared a moment
that I could turn to during my darkest days. In the months
following, I experienced a therapeutic breakthrough in the
form of visualization, giving me insight that I hadn't
previously experienced. At that time, I knew I had to find a
voice, and I decided to become a volunteer presenter. I was
willing to share my story of hope with anyone who would
listen. The final five poems highlight the process by which I
was able to claim control of my life, perhaps for the first
time.

The Wind Blows

A star moves across sky's black landscape
A new discovery in the darkness of my mind
As sudden as the star begins to soar
Light calls me within a dream to make a wish

A cool breeze begins to blow
Gently shaping my empty thoughts
And scattering them into a starlit night
In a world within a world.

The star descends from the sky
And time moves ever slower
My wish races against an inescapable truth
That I am haunted by the cruelty of chance

When the star nears earth
I wish the strengthening wind
Will carry my fears to safety
Within its soft, subtle embrace

Conversation of Souls

It was in the very moment I saw her,
Her hair was radiant with golden shine,
Wrapping the contours of her face,
Curling just beneath her chin;
Her eyes were a darker shade of brown,
Allowing me to see inside her spirit,
Telling me she was hiding from herself;
Her true beauty lie deep within,
Diminished by her finest qualities;
Was it love I sought from her?
Or a kindred spirit whose life was a mirror
That provided a reflection of my own
For a moment my heart touched hers,
I don't know if her heart grasped mine,
But I loved her in that instant,
Transient and passing moment of time;
I have never felt so alive,
As in that blissful sweetness,
Of souls calling to each other

*This poem honors the first time Cristl and I went out. The memory of this
moment still provides a light in my darkest times.*

I Visualize Myself in the Ocean

I surrender to the clear, calm waters
Conscious of life's meaning
My past shipwrecked and set adrift
The future faded into salty abyss

A gentle wave gathers strength
Crashes softly on the sandy beach
Dampened by the ocean's waters shaded white
And caresses my soothed bare feet

My eyes follow the ocean's currents
Aware of the moment's impermanence
The moon's grip steady as it rises and falls
Demonstrating the beauty of the living Earth

Truth lies in this vivid scene
That tranquility would be found
Evoking life's most disquieting questions
In the shadows of winter's long, cold embrace

This poem is written in honor of the important work performed by thousands of therapists and mental health workers, who save countless lives each day.

A Prayer for Strength

Allow my voice to rise above affliction
Let my will thread a needle through the tapestry of time
May I light within the lost the depths of conviction
A fire exists within by whose truths I must abide

Let none other than my oppressors misconceive
Beneath a river the current gains momentum
To those who listen I will not deceive
I will inspire a flood of hope to rise from the rains

My true colors have altered their tone
My fate I can no longer bemoan
I ask never to walk alone

May my emotions not change like tides of the sea
May I never reach the pinnacle of what it means to be

This poem is written in memory of all those who have lost their lives to suicide.
I know my fight is not for me alone but for you as well.

A Prayer of Thanks

I may have lived in eternal night
In darkness I witnessed the light;
The candle flame cannot last forever
The flame will be extinguished then lit again;
I have embraced death and been reborn
A new chapter I must amend;
The sun kisses me with its warmth
Still there are storms that I must contend;
I experience my first real smile
Gratitude will be shown to family and friends

About the Author

David Stant has been suffering from depression for most of his adult life. His struggles began during his sophomore year at the University of Maryland. He returned to his studies at Frostburg State University where he earned Dean's List honors three consecutive semesters and graduated with suma cum laude honors. David eventually found his calling as a non-profit mental health coordinator. He has been writing for the last ten years and has been published in Maryland Bards Poetry Review 2020 and Train River Poetry Anthology Summer 2021.

www.ingramcontent.com/pod-product-compliance
Lightning Source LLC
Chambersburg PA
CBHW060659280326

41933CB00012B/2252